SPIRITUALITY AND SUCCESS

A Guide to Using Spirituality for Success at Home and Work

SAVINDER PURI

An imprint of
Srishti Publishers & Distributors

Srishti Publishers & Distributors
A unit of AJR Publishing LLP
212A, Peacock Lane
Shahpur Jat, New Delhi – 110 049

editorial@srishtipublishers.com

First published in India by
Blue Rose Publishers in 2018

First published by Launchpad,
an imprint of Srishti Publishers & Distributors in 2024

10 9 8 7 6 5 4 3 2 1

This is a work of non-fiction, based on the author's thorough research and experience. While due care has been taken to verify all information at press time, any inadvertent miss brought to notice shall be updated in the subsequent editions.

Dedicated to the Light,

whose infinite wisdom is

humbly received and penned here

Foreword

"This beautiful book is a miracle by itself - just how Savinder's phone call came to me one winter afternoon of 2020, looking for answers for his wife. I was the last name on his list. It was meant to be.

Savinder's wife became my client and in her healing sessions, a strong message came through that Savinder needs a session as well.

After Savinder's session, he started taking his spiritual journey seriously. Going deeper, his purpose of life started unfolding. In due course, while navigating the challenges on the spiritual path, he was gifted with the ability of Automatic Writing (a form of Channelling from Higher Self).

As he learnt to listen to the 'callings', Higher Self started providing Spiritual downloads.

In a deep Theta state, Savinder filled pages after pages with the guidance provided.

Thus, this book was "written".

Savinder is special and he is here to help, serve and open up a certain side in the human blocks, including self-limiting belief systems, especially for people in his field of work (Corporate and IT firms).

I must say that when the student rapidly evolves in front of the teacher, it's one of the proudest moments for the Teacher! My blessings and Prayers will always be with Savinder. There is so much more to come through him for people who are lost and in need of guidance. This book is just the beginning!

Sending Savinder lots of love, light and abundance in his path to keep shining high and helping humanity become the best version of themselves

Nikki Dutta

Nikki Dutta is an International Psychic Medium and a Spiritual Teacher.

Her main purpose in this lifetime is "Expansion of Consciousness"- to teach & help humankind.

Nikkis is an Operational Remote viewer from ECRV (US), certified NLP and CBT Therapist and a QHHT Practitioner.

She has taught in London College of Pyschic studies. She's a Certified Advanced Medium from her mentor Gordon Smith.

You can reach her at https://thetranquility.co.uk/

To My Guru, Nikki

Words fail to express the profound gratitude I hold for you. From the moment our paths crossed, it was meant to be.

Under your loving guidance, both Manpreet and I started our transformations, awakening to the magic of spirituality.

Your unwavering dedication and belief in me enabled me to embrace my purpose and explore new horizons.

Your wisdom and compassion created a safe space for growth, empowering me to transcend limitations and step into my own power.

Nikki, I am forever indebted to you.

As I embark on this endeavor to share the wisdom of spirituality and success with the world, I carry your teachings deep within my heart.

You have ignited a fire within my soul, and I am committed to serving others with love, compassion, and integrity.

With eternal gratitude, for this lifetime and others,

Savinder

Contents

Introduction

**Everyone is a spiritual person,
whether you acknowledge it or not.**

**Everyone wants to succeed,
in their careers and home.**

The question is:

- *Can spirituality and success co-exist?*

- *Does spirituality have a place in today's fiercely competitive workspace?*

- *Can spirituality help in creating a happy home?*

- *Can you use the principles of spirituality to succeed in your career & parenting?*

This book seeks to explore such answers.

It is a humble attempt to crystalize the knowledge received through meditation and thought, and to put it out there for the world to consume.

This book is written by and for the Light.

I am just the medium who put the words on paper.

The book will help us understand and get aligned to Light work, which takes us closer to The Source.

Those who are ready to read this book, will get it.

Someone will recommend it to you...

You will "*happen to*" read about it somewhere...

Someone will talk to you about it.

The book will find you when you're ready.

Such are the mysterious ways of working of the universe!

So, if you've picked up this book, know that it's not by chance.

There is a bigger purpose to it.

While reading this book, you can either directly jump to a section that resonates, or read end-end.

It's yours to consume and adopt.

Give it the time and effort it deserves.

Because you deserve it.

Spirituality

**Spirituality is a connection with Higher Self,
a knowing of someone/something greater than oneself.**

**It's a feeling of One-ness,
the feeling that you are not alone here,
the feeling that you are being looked after.**

It's a knowing deep within that no matter what you say or do
in the outside world,
you are being watched and observed, in a loving and caring
way.

You might fool the entire world on how you behave or how
you act, but not yourself.
You know that you know.

**Once you being to understand and accept this
connection with Spirituality,
life starts to unfold rather interestingly.**

If you allow it to unfold like it's supposed to be, and not intervene at every step.

If you learn to listen to the little things and hints that are coming your way.

If you just sit back and enjoy the ride.

I have personally experienced this connection as I have let life unfold.

And I say this with all the humility - it's been a rather good life!

It's not all been a bed of roses, I can promise you that.

But it's been a life worth looking back at and worth thinking about and worth cherishing.

And we're just getting started here!

Spirituality is not some mumbo-jumbo magic trick.

It's not a veiled sequence of steps to help you get what you want.

It's not conniving with the Higher power to maneuver things your way.

In fact, it's quite the contrary – it's allowing yourself to be maneuvered in alignment with the Higher Self.

Spirituality is not some devious master plan to succeed in your career by "getting around" others.

It is not a strategy to get that million-dollar home you want.

It is not about manipulating relationships and people at home to your advantage.

It is not about always keeping *"just my family"* first.

In fact, it's quite the contrary.

It's about ***"Vasudhaiva Kutumbakam"*** – a Sanskrit phrase from ancient Indian scriptures which means ***"the whole world is one (my) family"***.

**If the entire world is my family,
then how can I manipulate my own family?**

Spirituality is perhaps the new recipe for world peace ☺

Spirituality for Success
In Your Career

How do you measure Success in your Career?
This is a rather difficult question to answer.

And that's because there is isn't a common definition for success – it means different things to different people.

- For some, success is financial.

- For others, it's the position and the intrinsic power that comes with it.

- For a few, it's the impact they can make in this world.

- For almost all, it's the feeling of contentment of having a day well lived, when the head hits the pillow at night!

These definitions of success also change over time.

As we grow and gain (or lose) more understanding of this world, our perspectives change.

Sometime, for the better. Sometimes not.

It is important to know what success in career means for You.

**And then, to figure out
how your definitions could get in alignment with the
Higher Self.**

If you already have (or want to create) your definition of success in career and home, read on and be ready to be amazed!

An important aspect of success is the price paid for the success.

WHAT DID YOU HAVE TO LOSE,
TO BE SUCCESSFUL?

We have all seen and read about people who are super successful in their careers. Perhaps, we even know some of them personally. We aspire to be certain versions of these successful men and women.

Being successful is a rather tricky, tight-rope-walk thing.

If you succeed in certain areas of your life,

and fail (or not so successful) in others,

what is the sum total?

Let's study some "hypothetical" success metrics…

1. *You became a CEO, and "lose" your family, because they do not care about you anymore (other than for the money, which is their right anyways!);*

2. *You get that big fat promotion but lost those two close friends from college, because you were not there for them when they needed you the most;*

3. *You move to another country to further your career and drag your spouse and kids with you, and they hate it there, every single day. Even the good money is not making them happy;*

4. *You won an amazing deal that turned the entire balance sheet of the company, yet you feel miserable since you know you did some not-so-right-things to win the deal;*

5. *You finally move into that big four-bedroom apartment you bought, yet it does not seem like home. You're always worried about the EMI and what if something happens to your job/business?*

6. *Just getting up every day feels life a drag and you especially dislike Monday mornings;*

7. *You just updated LinkedIn with your new title and realize that none of the people congratulating you are the ones you care about. These are all "connections", without the real connection. Just three of the college*

friends are in there. What about the other 36 from your graduation Class?;

8. *You have 487 friends in Facebook and 1689 followers in twitter. And yet you wonder - who are these people?;*

9. *You wake up on a lazy Saturday afternoon and wonder – how come no one calls me anymore?*

   I mean, call me, not for work or to wish happy birthday.

   Call me for the banter

   Call me just for the heck of calling me!

Did You Really Succeed?

If you read the previous chapters and it did not disturb you even a bit, read it again.

Read it like you own it.

This is a random sentence to tell you that you should stop reading and reflect.

Take a pause and let the previous sentence sink in.

If you're still reading this,

STOP!!!

Spirituality gives you an elusive wholesomeness.

Spirituality gives you the understanding that you do not have to lose anything to gain success.

SUCCESS SHOULD NOT BE AND IS NOT A BARTER SYSTEM.

A barter is how it has come to be most of the times, through that's not how it was originally designed.

Success is supposed to be fun

Success is supposed to feel like fun, right down to your bones. When you are striving towards it and even as you start striking down those milestones.

Your success does not have to be built on other's failures.

There is no dearth of success in this world — there is enough for everyone to go by.

And with your success, a lot of others should achieve their own little successes.

That's what adds the fun to it.

That's what makes the celebrations endure.

And spirituality allows you to do this, and more.

Is spirituality the perfect pill?
I believe so.

Have I achieved this?

It's work-in-progress.
But it's progress in the right direction.

Can you do this?

Why not… read on!

Spirituality For Success As A Home Maker

As I was writing this book, I requested my wife, Manpreet, to have a read of the initial chapters and give her inputs. She suggested – *"Why stick to success at Corporate – why not add the home maker angle to it as well?"*

Surely, a home maker works as hard (perhaps more) as compared to office goers? And success as a home maker is as critical as Corporate.

Couldn't agree more with her!

Success at home is even more important since that's where you *"return to in the end".*

If the home isn't a happy home – then, is it all really worth it?

A home maker essays several roles during a day – manager, builder, finance controller, chef, teacher, friend, mother, wife etc.

Surely, a home maker needs the right thought process to make all this work and make it work with the right intentions and vibrations.

Because his/her thought process gets passed on to the entire household and becomes the vibration of the home.

Have you even wondered how when you go to someone's house and it "just feels good"?

You even say — "your house has a great vibe".

This *"vibe"* of a house is not due to the size of the house or how many rare and expensive artefacts they have…

it's about the intentions and the energy of the house.

And that takes learning and doing things — using spirituality for success as a home maker.

Enduring Success With Spirituality

So, you now understand the importance of spirituality at your Career and Home.

You understand the concept of enduring success and how that's probably the elusive mantra you were looking for.

You are fascinated by all of this and want to get started ASAP.

Congratulations, you've accomplished step one!

You now know the final goal.
You know what you need.

You might not still fully understand the ramifications of this goal, but you've made the right beginnings. You've taken the first step.

Now is the time to celebrate.

To cherish this understanding.

Because it's the little things and understandings that count.

It's the little things that build the big ones!

**Take an evening off from work —
no office calls, no meetings.**

If possible, take a day off from work. Switch off the phone.

Request your spouse/partner/soul mate to do the same.

Both of you have something important to discuss, that potentially might change your entire lives.

It deserves the attention of one day/evening, at the very least.

Go out to a nice scenic place. By a river, at a farmhouse, at a garden, under a big tree — whatever relaxes you.

Or just sit in that cozy nook of your house.

Call upon your spouse/partner/soul mate.

If you're not in a relationship at this moment, just be with yourself.

You are and should be your biggest friend.

Explain to your spouse/partner/mate your new understanding.

Tell him/her on what you are set out to do.

Include him/her in your plans and share your excitement.

Help him/her understand why this is so important for you and why you're so excited about it.

Relish this moment.

Get a good drink. Have some good food.

Spend some quality time together.

You might get the question – *"so, how do we actually include spirituality to get success in career and home?"*

Be candid and say –
"I do not know that yet. But I will.
Because it's the right thing to do.
And I want to do it".

You do not need to know all the answers.

What is important is that YOU BELIEVE!

BELIEVE that you're on the right divine path,
for the highest good and that the answers will come to you,
in their own time.

When crossing a tunnel, you do not have to see your entire way out.

You just need to believe that you're on the right path that leads to the other side and see the next 2 steps. That's all that matters.

And before you know it, you will be on the other side – 2 steps at a time.

Trust in The Source,

The Greater Good,

The Higher Power…

WHATEVER YOU CAN TRUST IN!

Have a go at this alternate thought process.

Absorb this, understand this.

Talk about it, with your partner or with yourself.

BELIEVE, RINSE, REPEAT

In our personal journeys, when I and Manpreet started out on our spiritual path, we did not know where we were headed or even how to get "there".

We just took one step at a time, the step that felt right.

We trusted the process.

And in hindsight, we kept meeting one Spiritual person after another, one teacher after another – and they all had an important part to play in our journey. And here we are.

Like the wise one said:

"When the student is ready,

the teacher will appear."

The Power Of Intention

"You get what you intend to create by being in harmony with the power of intention, which is responsible for all of creation."

— Wayne W. Dyer, The Power of Intention: Learning to Co-create Your World Your Way

The first step was to know and understand what you want — to be successful in your career and home by using spirituality.

The next step is to intend doing so.

Intend not to anyone external, but to yourself.

To your true self.

We are always intending, whether we say it out loud or not.

Whether we are in the kitchen - intending to make coffee,
Getting ready for work - intending to have a great meeting,

On the way to work – intending to arrive in time,

In the parking – intending to find a spot,

Waiting for the elevator – intending that it's not full…

…we are always intending!

Intending positively and for the right outcome

Get into a cozy state of body and mind and set this intention
—

"I am successful in my career, home and life by using the principles of spirituality"

Repeat it out loud a couple of times.

Let you mind and your consciousness hear this loud and clear.

Close your eyes and focus on your breath.

Repeat this process a couple of times, until it feels right.
You will know.

There is no magic formula to this.

There's no secret.

You got to know, that you know, that you believe this.
This is how you are going to live your life, starting right now.

This is how you set your intention.
Simple.

End this process with a big, deep smile.
A smile that comes from your heart.

The smile you can feel, not just see in the mirror.
A smile that makes you smile!

Wonder at the beauty of it all and what's going to ensue in your life, for your highest good.

And don't forget that big smile!

Power Of The Spoken Word

Whom do we talk to the most?

Is it your partner,

your colleagues,

friends,

or someone at your place of worship?

IT'S YOURSELF.

We talk to ourselves the most.

And researchers estimate that as much as 70%of what we tell ourselves is negative...

- *"I don't like this dish",*
- *"My boss is the worst",*
- *"My house is so dirty",*
- *"Don't think I can do this",*
- *"No one really likes me",*
- *"I look too fat in this dress",*
- *"There's always too much work in this job",*
- *"What is wrong with my life?"*

If you resonate with the above,
is it a surprise that most of our actions deliver a negative
result?

If the input is 70% negative, how can the output be a – whole – lot – positive?

Medical researchers have told us that 75% of our illnesses are self-induced.

Several years back, I read a book called *"What to say when you talk to yourself"* by Shad Helmstetter.

In this book, Chad talks about the **"mental programming"** and that **77% of everything we think is negative, counterproductive and works against us.**

This negative programming that we all received (and continue to receive) has come to us quite unintentionally.

It has come to us from our parents (who wanted to protect us), it has come to us from our brothers and sisters, from our schoolmates, our associates at work, our life mates, advertising of all sorts, the newspaper and the news and social media.

We took all this negative programming to heart.

Year after year, word by word, our life scripts were etched.

**Layer by layer, nearly indelibly,
our self-images were created.**

In time, we ourselves joined in.

We began to believe what we were being told by others – and what we were telling ourselves – was true.

Repetition is a convincing argument.

Eventually, we believe what others told us and what we tell ourselves the most - we began to live out the picture of ourselves we had created in our minds.

Ok, so, what do we do — is it all gloom and doom?

Fortunately, not.

Being a software programmer by profession,

I know one thing about programming — it can be re-programmed!!

The re-wiring is hard and painful, especially if it's been formulated over years, but it can be done. Bit by bit, every single day.

I once heard in a webinar — *"how do you make a jar of black paint appear white?"*

1. Stop adding black paint
2. Keep adding more and more white paint.

It will go from black to dark grey to light grey and eventually white.

That's exactly what we must do:

Stop adding the black paint,

Start adding more and more white paint.

This is how Manpreet and I have stopped our negative programming, over the years:

1. **Stop newspaper:**

    We've been a newspaper free home for over a decade now. When my parents visit, the first thing my dad does is to subscribe to it for the period of their visit!

    All of my friends and colleagues know about this, and you'd be surprised about how proactive they are on sharing *"breaking news"* with me!

    I'm a firm believer – you will know what you need to know!

2. **Stop TV:**

    We have a TV but no cable. No crazy, pre-programmed content that's continuously ramming the brain.

    We only use streaming services like Netflix, Amazon, Curiosity Stream etc., where we can carefully choose the content to consume.

    What freedom!

3. **Controlled social media:**

    We spend a lot more time on Twitter and LinkedIn as compared to Facebook, Instagram, TikTok and such.

    It's more important to know what "real" people are saying about topics that I relate with, than "my friends" vacation shenanigans!

We follow the folks who inspire us.

4. **Detox weekends:**

Every couple of months, we collect everyone's phone in the home and put it in a basket in the living room, on a Saturday morning.

The rule is simple – you get the phone only if it rings.

No checking social media, emails, WhatsApp etc. for the weekend. Use the phone as a phone… it's phenomenally liberating!

5. **Enjoy the romance:**

There is a lot of romance in going for a walk in the woods, watching the sun rise/set, having a cuppa tea with a book, watching the plants grow, listening the sounds of nature and so on and so forth. You get the drift!

As the jungle saying goes –

"If you cannot enjoy your own company,

imagine how boring you must be to others!"

So, in summary, here's how Manpreet and I have done our re-programming over the years:

- Stop newspaper

- Stop TV

- Controlled social media

- Detox weekends (every couple of months)

- Enjoy the romance!

We cannot recommend you enough to try this out.

If there's only one thingy that you must take away from this book, it's doing the above!

The Not-So Secret Thingy

Many have read the book, **"*The Secret*"** and seen the videos by Rhonda Byrne.

However, everyone that you talk to, has a different version of *"The Secret"* and how it works.

And that version usually rallies to their core belief system.

Whether they accept it or not.

Let me explain:

- If a person is inherently **non ambitions**,

  they take solace in the fact that "The Secret" tells them to *"ask"* and *"it shall be given"*.

  They focus on the *"ask"*, rather than the work combined with the *"ask"*.

- And then there are "**the enlightened ones**"... What's the point of all this ask anyways – it's all gonna go away one day.

  So, "The Secret" tells them to be satisfied with what they have and not even desire for more.
  Often times, this really comes from a place of deep complacency.

- Then, there are the "**affirmation avocados**":
    o   An affirmation on their car mirror;
    o   On their laptop;
    o   At their desk;
    o   Of course, on their fridge;

- o   And all around the house
- o   They are a walking, talking affirmation!

Do all these guys believe in their affirmations? Of course they do!

49

But, do they take five minutes during the day to really feel and love their affirmation with all their heart – yes, they did that 3 months ago during that workshop where they were "taught" affirmation.

And it felt great that day.

And that's been enough to carry on and on.

Now, with all this going on –

why isn't everyone a millionaire yet?

Why isn't everyone living their best life yet?

Surely – something is amiss, somewhere…

Re-Booting Your Thought Process

While all books on Spirituality are great and should be read and practiced, there is a need to re-boot your thought process in addition to the reading.

Else, you will begin to create your own understanding and that may or may not work at the efficacy that it should and it can.

There is an algorithm to make your intentions more powerful and manifest what you REALLY REALLY want:

1. **Intend positively for the Highest Good**

2. **Intend in past/present, not in future tense**

3. **When putting intention, do not be attached with the outcome**

1. **Intend positively for the Highest Good**

Sometimes, we want something that is for our good only, not for the highest good.

We want it because we want it.

For e.g., let's say that a near one is sick and has been suffering. We love them dearly and do not want them to go. Our intention at that time is that this person continue to live, because that's what we want. And we start praying about it and affirming it.

But, what if, it's the last for this person?

What if, this person has decided to leave because they are going through a lot in their body and it's time for them to leave.

Maybe, he/she is not able to depart due to your intentions and prayers. Maybe, you are holding him/her back. Perhaps, it's not on us to decide the time, it's for their own highest good.

The right way to do this is the ask for the Collective's highest good.

Whatever is best, should happen.

The right way is this — intend positively for the Highest Good.

2. **Intend in past/present, not in future tense**

    When creating affirmations, do not say –

    "I will have it"

    Say, "I have it",

    "I receive… ", or

    "Thank you for granting me…"

    The science behind it is that you are bringing your frequency into the power in the NOW, already.

    When the frequency or timeline that is hovering around connects to the frequency or timeline that you want it, it becomes very easy to receive and manifest.

3. **When putting intention, do not be attached with the outcome**

This could be the biggest hinderance to the manifestation.

Say, I've intended something for the highest possible good, intended it positively, in the present tense and…

I am now completely thinking about it:

- o   *When will it happen?*
- o   *Why has it not happened yet?*
- o   *Is it even going to happen?*
- o   *Maybe, I did something wrong.*

You are putting YOURSELF in the middle of the intention and the result

If you've already affirmed in the present that this is already there, then why the self-doubt?

If you've already believed it, why the questioning now?

Let the outcome create itself.

Don't get in the way.

Believe – "BE" it and then, "LEAVE" it.

Why Do Intentions Not Manifest?

Let's say, I am intending something, this is for highest good, not just for me. I did not keep thinking about the outcome.

Yet, it did not happen.

What happened?

Remember, we said it's for the highest good.

Sometimes, what we really want, we intend with ego.

We are not open or awake to understand that these things are ever meant to be for us.

Maybe the universe has another plan for you.

Maybe a much bigger plan.

And you were thinking only that much at that time.

Give yourself some more time and it will always give you more understanding.

The more you grow into believing, the more you believe that you can let go of the outcome completely.

Even if it did not happen, it was not meant to be.

Maybe you are supposed to carry on.

Sometimes, we put a Date and time to the manifestation. That's fine too.

However, allow yourself a grace time without being impatient.

For us, the outcome becomes so important that we put some energies behind it that are not the highest vibrations that are required for manifestation.

Allow yourself time for things to materialize.

Some Practical Exercises For You

Let's say that as a home maker, you want to lose some weight.

First, let's look at all the factors that are important while losing your weight and add your specific asks on each:

1. *Current weight:* <aa> *kg*

2. *Target weight:* <bb> *kg*

3. *Target inch loss:* <xx, yy, zz> *inches*

4. *Date target:* <mmddyyyy>

5. *Why I want to lose weight: to stay healthy and makes me feel good about myself*

6. *What will I gain when I lose weight: self-confidence, smarter clothes*

7. *What do I want to do after I achieve my targets: Go and buy a bunch of new clothes!*

8. *What after that: Continue the new regimen, this is a lifestyle change and I want to make it permanent*

Now that you have the specifics nailed down, it's time to write down your intention.

Remember:

1. Intend positively for the Highest good

2. Intend in past/present, not in future tense

3. bringing your frequency into the power in the NOW, already

Ok, lets write down the intention now:

Thank you, God, for,

- *Helping me lose weight and inches and achieve my fitness goals*

- *By your grace, I have lost <nn> kg in <kk> months*

- *You have helped me achieve my first step of getting healthier so that I feel good about myself*

Dear God, I feel immense gratitude that

- *I feel so self-confident*

- *I love my body now*

- *I believe in my own opinions and do not get bothered by what others think*

- *Exercise and eating right is a lifestyle change that I have embraced, and I feel great about it!*

I am so ready to go out shopping with my best friend <name> today and get some awesome new clothes!

Thank you, thank you, thank you!!

Let's say, you're looking to change your job. How do you go about setting that intention?

First, let's look at all the factors that are important while changing your job and add your specific asks on each:

1. *Designation: Say - Director, HR Practice*

2. *Organization: FTSE 500 company*

3. *Salary: Say – GBP 130k/annum (USD 178k)*

4. *New job by when: <date>*

5. *Organisation values: <what's most important for you>*

6. *Location: Reading, UK*

7. *Boss: <describe his/her characteristics here>*

8. *Team: < describe their characteristics here>*

9. *Work: <what kind of work do you want to do>*

10. *Balance: <what will it take to find a good work life balance>*

11. *Growth prospects: <Two things that will excite you most about this job>*

Ok, lets write down the intention now:

Thank you, God, for,

- *Granting me a new job as Director, HR Practices at*

- *A FTSE 500 company <company-name(s), if you know it ready>*

- *With a salary of over GBP 130/year + 10% variable*

- *At Reading, UK, within 2 miles from the train station*

- *Starting from 15th Nov, 2023*

Thank you, God, for making sure that:

- ***My boss*** *is a very understanding person, technically competent in his/her area of expertise and supports his/her team all the time and gives credit where due. Is an easy person to talk to and provides strategic guidance as required*

- ***My core team*** *is a dynamic team, competent, full of joy and energy. They help each other and strive to get the job done, and get it done well. They work hard and party harder!*

- ***My extended team*** *is great at what they do and actively participate in all initiatives we launch and ensure each is a success*

Dear God, I love the fact that:

- ***I am getting to establish*** *HR Practices at a global scale and interact with Sr. Executives across multiple countries. This job has given me the opportunity to truly explore and express myself. Thank you for that.*

- ***I am able to*** *finish all my work by 5:00pm and return to my lovely home to play in the evening with the kids and spend time with my wife. I get the weekends to peruse my passion of bike repair and I'm getting all the parts I need easily. **Love the work life balance here!***

Thank you God for giving me a job that I totally love.

My growth prospects are through the roof and I am making the right impressions on the people that matter.

Every Project I touch is a success with accolades flowing in from the Senior Management.

All the people in my team are flourishing in their careers and that shows in the exemplary fashion in which they conduct themselves.

Thank you God for such a wonderful job.
Thank you, thank you, thank you!!!

Phew…

- Did you get goose bumps while reading this?
- Did you feel the energy in this?
- Could you already imagine your workplace?

Imagine, if you can repeat these kinds of well worded, deep intentions with all your heart – imagine what kind of vibrations you will create and imagine the power of manifestation!

Won't it be great if we can all create our "perfect" future, just like that.

Its indeed possible, just BE-LIEVE!!!

Make It Fun, Make It Sustainable

One of the biggest challenges of anything, especially these self-help category of things is this – how do you keep it sustainable and going in the long run?

All this manifestation, self-talk and affirmations may seem so cool in the beginning, especially if you do accomplish some things. The question is – how do I store and retain that feeling over a sustained period?

Especially, when things are not working out for me and when I'm having an especially bad day or week or more.

How do I keep going?

And through that week and that month?

There is a layered answer to this, one that connects at a very deep level.

1. **Why does it feel like things are not working out for you?**

   Because you thought of something, intended it deeply and that did not happen? Life is not going according to your plans?

   If all this sounds familiar, I would highly recommend you do three things.

   If you do these three things immediately, I promise you will get a totally different perspective, this very instant:

   - **Step 1:** Get up from where you are, and go get yourself a glass of water

   - **Step 2:** Look carefully at the glass of water, admire the wonderful creation of water and how beautiful it looks. Imagine a beach, a large swimming pool, a lake, a waterfall with all your heart and emotions. These are all manifestations of this water, the various ways in which this water expresses itself

   - **Step 3:** Say a small prayer of gratitude and drink the water!

   What we have done here is to shift the focus from You to God/creation/beauty.

   Shifted the focus from problem to solution and creation.

2. **Back to basics**

   Have a re-read of the chapter — *"Re-booting your thought process"*

   Really understand what's written there and absorb it.

   Now, have another read at the chapter — *"Why do intentions not manifest?"*

   Have a think about what you've just read

3. **Meditate and gain the understanding**

   Move into a quiet place of the house. Choose the right time of the day/night when you have about 30 min when no one will disturb you. Light an incense stick or put up a good perfume or use a de-fuser. Something to simulate your sense of smell.

   Put on some light meditation music, you can find several on YouTube.

   Put out the intention that you are seeking understanding of why *"are you stuck?"*.

   You are seeking to truly imbibe this understanding.

   Close your eyes and allow the information to come to you.

Trust the process and keep your eyes closed for 10 min, or as long as you want to keep them closed. Listen intently for any communication from the Beyond, with your ears and your mind. Listen hard.

It might appear that you are imagining this information and it's coming from your mind itself. That's ok, just trust the process and do it anyways. Take a note of whatever is coming through.

Stay seated for a couple of minutes more.

Relish the feeling.

Enjoy the experience.

4. **Make it fun**

Talk about what you've learned with your partner. Discuss the experience.

It's amazing what you can understand just by talking to someone else.

Just by saying things out loud.

Your own brain kicks into action and a "eureka moment!" just might happen.

Talk about this with the kids.

Involve them in the process.

Make them understand how to work this. Meditate together.

You will be surprised how easily kids understand and appreciate meditation!

Have fun.

Enjoy the process.

Quite often, we take this "intention business" a tad too seriously.

We tend to think of this as "grown up stuff".

Leave aside talking to anyone else about this, we seldom even discuss this with our partner. We take on complete responsibility of setting and getting intentions on our own.

This is a rather myopic, self-centered approach and leaves the family a very good and sustainable chance of learning and growing together.

And of being a family together.

A family is not just the one that eats or sleeps together – it's the one that struggles and celebrates together!

Here's what I would recommend — whether you are a home make or a Corporate person reading this - involve your partner into this intention thingy.

If possible, have them read this book to understand the context. If not, have them read the couple of relevant chapters.

If even that's not possible, re-think why they won't even spend 30 min on what you're asking them to do so fervently?

Explain to them what intentions are about, the thought process etc.

Read the two intentions given in the book and discuss them.

Understand them.

Absorb them.

Then, figure out what intentions do you want to set together.

Get a nice cuppa tea (of whatever floats your mojo!) and block about an hour for this exercise. This is important stuff; you are defining your future life here!

Create your intention:

1. Intend positively for the Highest good

2. Intend in past/present, not in future tense

3. Bring your frequency into the power in the NOW, already

Revisit the previous chapters and check if the wordings and tenses are correct.

Check if you've covered everything you want. Re-check

This is the most important document you will ever create.

This is the balance-sheet of your life.

Now, set about a regimen of how and when this intention will be said out.

As a fun thingy that we do very often in our home, involve the kids.

They are much better than us "adults" in understanding all of this, their minds are still mailable and not fixated on failure yet. Have them create small intentions for what they want in their lives.

Does not matter if it's a house or a toy house, the Universe works in the same way.

Time, space, money does not matter to the Universe, these are the constraints in our three-dimensional mind.

Another totally fun activity to be done with kids is — "creating vision boards".

If you're not sure what this means, I highly recommend pause reading and search for this in YouTube.

Get old magazines, books, newspapers in the house. We often struggle with this part since we do not have any of these things in the house (we stopped getting newspapers in the house, remember!!). We visit the local hawker and buy old magazines solely for the purpose of creating vision boards.

You will be amazed at the kind of magazines you will buy to create vision boards — these are typically stuff that you would not buy, since they do not seem "logical enough" to buy in the natural course of things. For e.g., I would very rarely buy a fashion or product catalogue magazine. But on this outing, these make perfect sense!!

Make this fun, involve the family.

Make it last.

It's your life creation after all, who would enjoy it if not you?

Overcoming A Difficult
Boss At Work

A word of caution before you read further — if you've just jumped to this chapter directly, read no further.

This is not a click-bait title, there's a reason why this chapter is where it is in the book.

You need to know, understand, and internalize a few things before you can use the information to be presented in this chapter, in the right context.

So, if you're serious about *"overcoming a difficult boss at work"*, invest a couple of hours or days to read through the book.

If you think if you have a serious situation at work, give it the seriousness it deserves.

Overcoming a difficult boss is more of a mental game than anything else.

As the first step, define the problem statement:

What about the boss is difficult?

- *Does he/she not value your work?*

- *Are you not treated well at work?*

- *Does he/she ridicule you in front of others or 1:1 with no fault of yours?*

- *Are you over being worked – either being assigned the tasks for multiple people or just too much to do?*

- *What else?*

- *Anything else that makes your boss a difficult boss?*

- *Are you sure there's nothing else?*

Often time, just taking the time out to list the above is a revelation.

What you thought was a huge mountain of a problem is actually only three things!

All the others were just thoughts in your mind, which you could not pin down on paper, even for your own consumption!

The tiger was appearing much bigger in the mind's eye, than it really is!

Next step, analyse the situation:

- *Does this happen only with you?*

- *Are there others who also share the same opinion about the boss?*

- *How often does this happen? Have there been one off instance that have troubled you or is this something that keeps happening, not even letting you sleep at night. Are you literally losing your sleep over this?*

- *How severe are the instances? How disturbed are you?*

- *Is this getting into the space of making you emotionally disturbed?*

- *Would you like to involve the HR in this? Has it reached a stage where your mental health is being impacted?*

If the answer to a lot of these is YES, please stop reading and start thinking about reporting this to the right people at work.

Even if it's not a formal complaint, there could be informal, even anonymous ways to report things at work. Perhaps they have a "complaint box/form" where you can post without your details. Perhaps you can talk to your HR "in confidence".

Perhaps another senior who has been in the system for a while and who can be trusted. Maybe something else. Think about it.

The most important thing is to protect your mental sanity at all costs.

By this time, you should have established the following about your _difficult boss_:

- _You really do have a_ **difficult boss**

- _It's not just you that he/she's_ **difficult** _with_

- _The situation is serious but not critical. It's not something that's taking an immediate toll on your mental health_

Great, now let's talk about some strategies on how to overcome a **difficult boss**.

Did you notice how many times _"difficult boss"_ is repeated in the above paragraphs?

1. Stop the repetition

Stop repeating to yourself that you have a difficult boss. Control that mental narrative. Stop discuss this with your colleagues at work. We have already established that he/she is difficult. Now is the time to do something about it, more than just fussing about it.

Now is the time to stop putting in the Black paint. Start putting in the white paint, but that won't work until you stop the flow of black one!

2. Start the intention

Well, now that you're armed with the power of intention (from previous chapters), use it. Create the best intention that you can, with all your emotions.

You already know how to manifest it, so go for it.

Follow all the steps and then believe!!

3. He/She is not the only ass**** in this world – deal with it!

One thought that often comes through - let me just quit this company.

It's even said – "people do not leave companies, they leave bosses".

However, I have a slightly different point of view:

- *What if the next boss is even more difficult?*

- *What if this one seems to be a cakewalk as compared to the new one?*

- *How do you know that the grass on other side is greener?*

Take a hard look at your circumstances before you decided to change the job.

In my experience of 20+ years, there have been at least five instances where I've had very difficult bosses – they checked all the above criteria. And yet, in all the instances, I've waded through the waters.

In a couple of months to a year, they either changed roles, relocated to a different are of business or just moved out of the organization. I waited them out. And it all turned out OK.

I survived and thrived, in the same organisation.

4. Changing expectations...

As you gain experience and progress in your career, the dimension and expectation of your boss also change:

- *At 2-3 years' experience, perhaps you were explicitly told what and how to do things*

- *At 5+ years' experience, maybe the boss just tells you "what" (to do) and expects you to figure out the "how"*

- *At 10+ years, perhaps you are expected to figure out the "what" as well ☺*

- *At 15+ years, perhaps the boss expects things "to just happen" and he/she is not to be bothered with the dirty details. All that's expected off you – is zero escalations*

You might not be ready for this kind of expectation change and might be stuck at the initial mindset – *"just tell me what to do and I will do it. But tell me!"*

5. The five love languages

Maybe, just maybe, a boss, like a lover, cannot express himself/herself.

He/she was not born a boss. They did not receive a formal training (most of them really do not!) and yet, here we are.

Perhaps, all of this is as simple as – they do not know on how to express themselves or how to ask what they want. And you're giving them something different. You both are talking different "love languages"!!!

I'm referring to this timeless book by Dr. Gary Chapman - <u>Discover Your Love Language - The 5 Love Languages®</u>

Dr. Chapman says – *"The premise of The 5 Love Languages™ book is quite simple: different people with different personalities give and receive love in different ways. By learning to recognize these preferences in yourself and in your loved ones, you can learn to identify the root of your conflicts, connect more profoundly, and truly begin to grow closer."*

A boss of mine several years ago did not like to listen to ideas. He would never ask – *"what do you think"?* Those words did not exist in his dictionary at all. And if you did butt in and told him what you thought, he would get very cross!

However, if he told you to do something and you did it differently, he would look at the merits of what you had done and then even accept it. But he did not like to be told of this beforehand.

In the end, the important thing was that he accepted what was right. The fact that he did not like to be told became *"tolerable"*, once I understood the reasoning for that!

Another boss of mine was a complete party person. He would invite folks from work at his home, have loads of alcohol with them and play cards. He would take everyone to these lavish dinners and splurge. He just wanted to be around people and share his stories. And he was even willing to pay for it!

A lot of people thought they "had to go" to these parties if they wanted to be "close" to him. They thought that if he saw them regularly at these parties, they would benefit at work.

I, however, took a different approach.

After attending one or two of these parties and realizing what the pattern is, I had a candid conversation with the boss. Told him that I would not be able to attend these parties because I want to spend time at home, I have other passions that I want to peruse post work, that this is just not something that aligns with my personal preference. I most respectfully declined (almost all) his future invites right there. And he was cool with that. He got it. And never forced me to come or reprimanded me for not joining.

He just wanted to feel accompanied and as long as he had enough people, he did not care about me not joining the gang.

It was about him; it was not about me.

6. Their frustration is not your frustration

Some bosses are genuinely frustrated with life. They just do not like the sun when its shining, the clouds when it rains and any weather in between. They are genuinely frustrated in life.

Do not let their frustration become your frustration.

Stay away from such people; they should not make it to your birthday party list!

Maintain distance from these bosses. Be strictly professional. If you are secure with your work and believe in that, do not worry about their frustration.

7. Secure yourself

Build allies in the organization. People should respect you for your expertise. Other seniors should acknowledge and appreciate your work. Find out opportunities to showcase your work to others and build that respect. Work for others out of turn, help them, invest your time. These investments will go a long way. There is a difference between "buttering someone" and "helping someone". Know that difference and stick to what you do best.

9. Network and secure yourself even more

There should always be three other roles/departments in the organization that you can transition into. And one senior person who wants you vocally in his/her team!

This is the situation where you want to be in. This is the sweet spot.

It takes time and effort to get here. Invest that time and effort.

10. Create visibility on LinkedIn, Twitter etc.

Be known in the community as an expert, or at least as an emerging expert. That can start today, it does not have to wait for anyone. Study the LinkedIn content game – what kind of content can I put out that will get the traction. Curation is a big thing these days… you do not have to create original content. Just curate what's already out there. And publish it.

For e.g. 5 ways to eat healthy, 3 tips to getting up early in the morning, 4 ways to read a book in 2 days etc. etc. This content is available out there, just collate it and publish on LinkedIn, Twitter etc. Content aggregation is a great idea.

11. Free yourself from the boss

Finally, you are not what the boss thinks. If you are secure, have built the right relationships, others want you in their teams – it's easier to free yourself from the boss.

"Forgive others, not because they deserve forgiveness, but because you deserve peace"

Once you reach this stage, you do not have to worry about overcoming a difficult boss… the boss will have to worry about you ☺

Managing Your Subordinates
(At Work)

Let's look at four perspectives of managing your subordinates:

1. **Subordinates are not your competition**

    The fact that you are a boss means that someone thought you were worthy to lead your subordinates – hopefully, both technically and emotionally. That does not mean you are technically the most superior. It means that you can get the best technical output from your team, using your emotional and leadership quotients (EQ and LQ). This is not manipulation; this is basic understanding of human need and desires and how to help them get it.

2. **Hire smarter than self**

    Lee Iacocca *(American automobile executive; best known for reviving the Chrysler Corporation as its CEO during the 1980s) once said,*

    "I hire people brighter than me and get out of their way."

    This is exactly what a leader is supposed to do – lead the subordinates and enable them to succeed. Your talent is not to be the best, it is to make the best work together. And that output would be greater than the sum of its individual best parts!

    This is easier said than done – but that's why great leaders are revered around the world and become stuff of legends!

3. **You cannot grow without them – superman flew alone!**

Superman is great, but flies alone! And it takes more than one excited superman to build and grow an Enterprise. Some would even argue that leadership is about creating more supermen and wonder-women in your team. And then, allowing them to blossom.

It really is a win-win, if you make it so

Happy subordinates make a happy organization and home.

And that makes the organization or home profitable – financially, emotionally and spiritually.

It really is as simple as that.

Managing Your Subordinates
(At Home)

As a home maker, do you identify with the following:

- *Are you someone who gets stressed when there is too much to do at home — when you see the piled-up dishes, the dirty kitchen, the unkept wardrobe and litter in the living area?*

- *Can you ignore all the mess and just watch a Netflix show? Or is this too discomforting for you to even enjoy your favorite show?*

- *Will you be able to sleep without "fixing" all this or do you have to put all things right even before you start thinking of sleeping tonight?*

If the answer to most of the above is a resounding yes, you are not alone.

Read on!

Let me introduce to the famous **Eisenhower Method** - categorizing tasks into whether they are:

- Urgent and whether they are important

- Recognizing that important tasks may not be urgent

- And urgent tasks are not necessarily important

	URGENT	NOT URGENT
IMPORTANT	**Quadrant 1** Urgent and important **DO**	**Quadrant 2** Not Urgent but important **PLAN**
NOT IMPORTANT	**Quadrant 3** Urgent but not important **DELEGATE**	**Quadrant 4** Not Urgent and not important **ELIMINATE**

Here's an illustration of the matrix to a common household.

Focus on box 2 - the items that are non-urgent but important.

These are the ones most people are likely to neglect, but should focus on to achieve effectiveness.

	URGENT	NOT URGENT
IMPORTANT	House on fire Baby crying Self care **DO**	Exercise Vacation Managing work **PLAN**
NOT IMPORTANT	Interruptions Home chores Repeatable work **DELEGATE**	Time wasters -ve influences Just being busy **ELIMINATE**

If all this is too technical or not your cuppa tea, do not worry.

Do not take further stress trying to understand the above!

Here's an alternate, less technical and more spiritually aligned explanation:

Let's focus on just four words:

- **Do**
  - What are the things that **you and only you** must do and do now?
  - Take care of them
  - **Celebrate them once done** – make a nice cuppa coffee and enjoy it. Watch TV for 15 min. Call a friend. Eat a biscuit. Complement yourself for a job well done. Smile!

- **Plan**
  - Plan your weekly meals and get the ingredients that you need to cook at on go. Do not make trips every day to get that one ingredient you need today. Plan.
  - Plan the school drop for the kid, start 5 min earlier so that you do not have to run to school. You can have a little banter with the child. Get that coffee on the way back and enjoy the walk or drive. Look at the nature around you, listen to that song on the radio, appreciate life!
  - Plan that Saturday party at your place. Think about what all you need and order earlier. Invest time in doing things on time so that they do not bubble up and become critical.

- **Delegate**

  - This is the most difficult thing to do. There's also perhaps an element of guilt associated with this one – if I let other do this, am I being a good wife/mother/daughter?

  - You are not super human, you cannot do everything. Get help. It's OK. People understand

  - Rather than burning yourself out, it's better to get help and then focus on things that you do best.

  - If you get someone to cook or clean the house periodically or to take care of the kids, that's perfectly fine

  - Need something sent somewhere – use a courier or delivery service. Do not waste your time. People understand

- **Eliminate**

  - If you take a serious look at everything that you do during a week, I'm sure there would be a couple of things that you can eliminate from your schedule, and thus gain time and peace. These are things that are just there, for no reason

  - Is it really necessary to spend 2 hours every day watching YouTube? Sure, it's important to relax, but 2 hrs??

  - If you were paid to do a million dollars to do just three things today, what would those three things be? Do you really need to do the rest? Can you do them tomorrow or not do them yourself at all, can you eliminate them?

  - Eliminate stuff and be free!

If this is still getting too complicated for you,

I have an even simpler mantra for you:

<u>Do what you feel like!</u>

What does that mean? Am I kidding?

Let me explain – let's say that there's lots of work to do around the house and you do not feel like making dinner tonight. Instead of making a hurried dinner and wrapping up the work as well – focus on what's causing you more stress – making dinner or tidying up?

Do one and take care of the other. Do the tidying up. Order in, have some leftovers or just cook up something really quick in the Owen. The important thing is that you took care of what was troubling you and you managed the rest. You did have a decent meal as well. The important thing was you did **<u>what you felt like</u>**!

If you feel right, you will live right ☺

Stress At Home Or Workplace

In our complicated lives today, it is seemingly "normal" to be stressed at home or in the workplace.

We all have that "nauseating" boss or (someone)-in-law who's breathing down our necks all the time, making life seemingly impossible!

It all looks rather hopeless at that time, with no way out at all.

And if the situation has been around for weeks/months/years, it looks even more incredibly difficult and "nauseating"!

You're not even sure how long you can carry on!

First, take a deep breath. Come on, do it now!

The fact that you're reading this chapter means that you want to do something to solve it.

And that's a good start, you've not given up – just yet!

Now, let's take a spiritual approach to the whole situation:

Accept the situation

This is the first step. As simple as it may sound, there are a couple of layers to this:

- Accept that the situation exists

- Accept that you are responsible for the fact that the situation exists (at least for your part of the situation)

- Accept that you must do certain things to deal with the situation

- Accept that not all things are in your control

- Accept that your sanity and happiness is absolutely in your control and that's the most important thing that counts

Remember the famous <u>Serenity Prayer</u>

God, grant me the serenity to accept the things I cannot change,

courage to change the things I can,

and wisdom to know the difference.

Remember what we've learnt earlier

Conventional wisdom would state that once you accept the situation, create a plan on how to handle it. Break down the problem into smaller parts and then try and work on them – solve the problem bit by bit.

If this works for you, great!

Chances are, you've already tried this approach and it either did not work at all, or created 5 more difficult situations ☺

Let's look at an alternate thought process.

A spiritual thought process.

Remember, from our previous chapters on create your intention:

1. *Intend positively for the Highest good*

2. *Intend in past/present, not in future tense*

3. *bringing your frequency into the power in the NOW, already*

Believe, rinse, repeat.

We follow the same process here as well.

While you're doing the intention stuff, it's important to let go of the outcome and the timelines.

Things will happen when they are meant to happen.

While this may sound oddly frustrating to read, once you start practicing it, it's rather liberating.

It's like – I've done my part, now it's up to HIM (God / Life Force / Energy / Universe – whatever you believe in).

The onus on getting the result is not on you anymore.

Coupled with the firm belief that things will happen for your highest good, having done your part already, it's fascinating to "watch" as the future unfolds.

You can almost marvel at the turn of events and be in awe of how things pan out.

And you will know that whatever happened was not a coincidence, it was all ordained.

Let go and let live.

Work Life Balance

It has getting more and more fashionable to say – *"Sorry, but I'm busy at work"*.

That I do not have time to indulge in exercise, the kid's basketball game or just watch TV with the family. And in this age of the pandemic, when the boundaries of work and home have blurred, this is even more plausible. Because work has come home, and it isn't set to leave anytime soon!

If you are a home maker, you can be in the same boat too.

You have that cleaning to do, that laundry to take care of, those almirahs to organize, those holidays to plan… you are pretty busy yourself and do not have the time to sit with kids to watch that show or to sit with your partner and participate in his/her game night.

The entire "work life balance" idiom is oversold.

There is no balance, it's harmony.

One thing is meant to flow into another.

They are meant to be complimentary, not competitive.

Because you must work or complete the household chores, you do not have time for family – this is not a valid argument.

These are not competing priorities.

These are complimentary.

You have to do both.

That's what makes a harmonised life.

It's not balanced life because there really is no balance. It's not perfect. The scales are not equally aligned on both sides. It's a moving target each day to find that harmony. One day, a particular musical note is higher, other days both the notes are at all time high. Yet, there is a harmony in all of this, if you listen carefully and craft the harmony so!

Now, how do you achieve this harmony?

Focus on what's important and critical. Do that. Take care of it.

Let things not escalate. Finish that presentation for the Customer meeting. Complete that proposal. Work on that critical monthly work update. Do the washing and cooking so that there's clothes to wear and food to eat.

Work late if you have to. Stretch into the night, wake up early. Burn the midnight oil. Enjoy it. Break the balance; create harmony.

Also, find time for that family TV show. Sneak in the game. Pause the "work" at that time. Turn off that washing machine for 30 min, the machine is not going to feel bad!

Do not let work-from-home become only-work-from-home.

This is a fundamental change you have done to your lifestyle since mankind stopped hunting and stating going out for 9-to-5 jobs.

Work on it and make it work.

There is no balance, there is only harmony.

One thing is meant to flow into another.

They are meant to be complimentary, not competitive.

It's All Hard Work

All that you've read till now is all hard work.

It's not some wishy-washy stuff that you can start doing from Monday morning and expect results by Wednesday.

This will take deliberate efforts to start and then continue the path.

It will take a conscious effort to stay on this mental path and gradually change the very DNA of your being. It's all hard work.

And why not – the use of spirituality to succeed in your career and home is not even seen as a combination today.

It's a new concept that we're bringing about.

It's almost like a new revolution.

But if you ask yourself honestly – what choice do you really have?

To understand it deeper, here's the chronology of birth since the late 40's. – the generations that we can still see on the face of the planet:

- *Baby boomers (born between 1946 and 1964) is over, they are currently between 57-75 years old.*

- *Gen X (born between 1965 and 1979/80) are currently between 41-56 years old*

- *Gen Y or millennials (born between 1981 and 1994/96) are currently between 25 to 40 years old*

- *Gen Z is the newest generation (born between 1997 and 2012) are currently between 9 to 24 years old*

- *Gen A or Alpha (born in 2012 and will continue through 2025)*

There are changing proprieties and thought process for each "generation".

The Baby boomers and Gen X had a mentality of scarcity and security, they stuck to their jobs and saved their entire life. There wasn't much to go around, and it was all very hard to get. Getting a job and sticking to it was the thing. Making one home in a lifetime and securing it was the thing.

Gen Y grew up in an age where the economies of the world were opening up, where abundance was creeping out of the confines. People were earning well and thinking about the nicest things in life. Home started becoming an investment and people today have multiple homes. Things started to open up and the thought of abundance was sown.

Gen Z came into a world where internet was already a thing. Where international travel was common place. Where the basics of food and shelter was already taken are of. Where the needs were much beyond the necessities and shifted towards significance of life. *"Who am I and what am I doing here"* became a dominant question.

Gen A or Alpha: A large part of this generation are being brought up through the pandemic. Things like masks, vaccination, global warming etc. are part of their daily conversation. It's about saving the world now and making an impact. The world is becoming a smaller place and the definition of home is changing.

What happens in one part of the world has a tangible and direct impact on another seeming unrelated part. We were never as close as this earlier.

As the focus of todays and future generations transitions from self to others and then to the world, there is a greater need for spirituality to rise and provide collective intelligence.

It is acting as the life-force and guiding light to this new age of indigo and theta kids.

The symphony of life is now more important than ever.

It's not enough to have a great job or a happy home.

Having both is the need.

And rightly so, that's the whole point of life.

To enjoy the niceties of life here on this planet.

Find that balance here itself, build it and cherish it.

Make the example and demonstrate it for the world to see.

Tell your story and write that book to inspire others to live their best life now!

Because we deserve it this way.

Expand Your Persona

Go for a job interview today and you are expected to have five skills – and an expertise level in most of them.

They need a ninja or superman/wonder woman to do the job.

Talk to a home maker and they are cooking multiple cuisines (almost like a master-chef), designing the home (almost like an interior designer) and managing finances and investments (almost like a professional accountant).

It takes a ninja or superman/wonder woman to do the job.

And with the new understanding that we have - we want the best of both work and home for us! We want the harmony to exist and a happy place where values for kids are "caught" and not "taught".

It's like packing the agenda of a couple of generations into one generation!

Like they say – "Lord, give me patience and give it now!!" ☺

All this needs an increase of consciousness and expansion of the Persona.

Operating at the older level of awareness is not going to be helpful.

There must be a shift in the fundamental DNA.

Expanding your persona is easier than you thought.

Acceptance

It starts with an acceptance of the new world.

A world where the collective wrong matters, where you develop your capabilities to "see and hear things" and where you can tap into the future and carve it out.

Where miracles a part of your daily life and not a once-in-a-lifetime occurrence.

Where you operate at a higher frequency and are *"in-tune"* with the Light.

Seek the truth

Once you accept what you want, then you go out and seek the truth. You prepare yourself to receive it and keep your eyes and ears open.

You might see something on TV or Netflix, read in an article online or someone even might just say something directly to you.

Be open to receive the information and you will receive it. Just tune into the frequency of Light and the voice will come through.

I got told to write this book for a couple of months. At first, it was slight, nudging message. I would read about a new author that won an award, a new publisher that has sold a million copies, a survey about a new book would pop up in LinkedIn etc. It was the gently push to me to start writing.

And then, the messaging grew louder and louder!

These synchronicities started happening more and more – everywhere I go, I would hear the word "book". It was all very amazing, funny and annoying at the same time. And then, 2 or 3 "random people" just talked up to me and asked – *When are you writing your book?"*

Understand the truth

Once you start recognizing the synchronicities, spend some time to understand them. Everything happens for a reason. Understand the reason. Meditate on it. Think about it. Ask to understand the truth - it will all come through.

I knew that I had to write this book and write it now… I started thinking about the title. Put out the intention that I'm looking for the title and the table-of-contents. Asked my spirits and higher guides for help.

Work the truth

You can meditate and think all you want, it ain't gonna matter if you do not do the work.

I started putting the alarm for 5:00am every day and started getting up at that time as well. The very first day, I got the entire Table of contents written down in under 20 min!

And since then, I've been waking up at 5:00am every single day. And for several days now, even before the alarm. No matter what time I sleep. There's the power of working the truth.

For context, I'm a night owl. Most active from 1:00 to 3:00am, when the entire world is asleep. That's my full energy zone. And yet, I'm now getting up at 5:00am and still feeling on-top-of-the-world!

Believe the truth

In this area, there are no example to look at. All of it is new. And the "imposter syndrome" is really easy to set it — "Who am I to go all this? Am I really good enough? What's so special about me"

When this starts happening, go to step one and repeat.

Do — rinse — repeat!!

Centering Yourself

As you engage in the practices illustrated in this guide, you will start turning into a different person.

You will have clarity of thought that you never had, people will become magnetically attracted to you and will want to talk and spend time with you since you radiate a different kind of energy.

Opportunities will open up that never even existed in the first place.

You will smile or start singing, for no apparent reason at all.

You will be happy, for no apparent reason at all.

Your soul will be happy – and you will know that you know.

One important thing to do at this time is to "center yourself".

To return to the core of your being, so that the peripheries can be chaffed off.

To ease the process, to help the Universe do this.

The art of Centering is simple – like everything else in nature.

It will take ten min to start with and yet these will be the best ten minutes of your life. Every single day.

Here's what you do:

1. *Get your phone with headphones/ear pods etc.*

2. *Go you YouTube, Spotify of your favorite media streaming application*

3. *Search for "10 minute guided meditation" – there are tons of these on You Tube*

4. *Pick the one that you resonate with. You will like one just looking at the thumbnail. Do not over-engineer this process and listen to 10 to pick one. Trust yourself – select the first one that your finger selects!*

5. *Sit in a comfortable posture, or lie down*

6. *Start the guided meditation*

7. *Enjoy the experience*

8. *Once the meditation is over, take your time to get up*

9. *Ease into this world slowly, you've just returned from a magical land!*

10. *Have a glass of water*

11. *Once you're back, go about your work*

Do this centering exercise for ten days and then notice the difference.

You will feel at ease with yourself and the world around.

You will find yourself looking for longer meditations and non-guided ones as well, at times.

Once you're found the center and eased into it, you will feel the safe zone around it.

This is your adobe – in unison with the universe.

Return to this at least once every 24 hrs to recharge and renew.

You will get such wonderful ideas about work or home after this exercise!

Your mind will be the mind of God ☺

What If All This Does Not Work?

Ok, this one is for the pessimists out there!

Firstly, let's be honest – there is some incredible stuff in here, don't you agree?

Even though some of it might seem wild and too-good-to-be-true, it is fascinating, right?

So, lets imagine a scenario.

You got hold of this book (really, you think that's just a coincidence? Think again!?)

You got hold of this book, read it through and tried some of the suggestions mentioned here.

And nothing worked.

Like nada.

No effect, you did not get anything through it.

At some chapters in the book, you could not even relate to what was written.

Right off the bat, you knew the chapter was not for you.

You even found some of the suggestions mentioned as totally outrageous – things just do not happen like this in your world.

Fair enough.

So, now what?

You "wasted" about the cost of a coffee… or probably not even that much!

It's just one of those things that did not work out.

What's the big deal?

It's not like you invested a million bucks and your investment tanked.

It's not like you spent 6 months on a course and now the technology is no longer relevant.

It's not like you spend 500 GBP on a new vacuum cleaner and now there are not going to be any cobwebs anymore in the world!

Ok, the last vacuum cleaner example was a little jaded, but you get the drift ☺

Now that you have a smile on your face, lets revisit the situation!

You did not get anything from the book.

If I can rephrase this – You did not get anything from the book, yet.

Recollect the guidelines to create your intention:

1.   Intend positively for the Highest good

2.   Intend in past/present, not in future tense

3.   Bring your frequency into the power in the NOW, already

The manifestation happens in HIS time, not yours.

Maybe, you are not to get this understanding today.

Maybe it's not your time yet.

Maybe, there some more things to be learnt first, some more growth to happen first, some more experiences to be had to make this understanding easier.

However, the seed has been sown.

Now, you know have been introduced to these concepts and know where to know about them.

Maybe, you will "casually" mention this book to a friend or on social media, maybe someone will pick that up and that person gains something awesome from the book.

Something that deeply impacts them, something they had been searching for a long time.

Maybe, you are just supposed to be a conduit in this case.

You job was to lead that other person to this book and that's it.

That was your play concerning this book in this universe.

You don't know what you don't know.

So, if you did pick up this book and did read this, know that it happened because of some divine reason.

It's not for you to understand that.

Its for you to be.

If you can use something from this book, that's great.

If not, HE will anyways have you use something from this book anyways!

EITHER WAY, THIS WORKED!

If this book made you feel good, recommend it.

If this book made you think, recommend it.

If this book made you feel uncomfortable, recommend it.

You may or may not agree with everything written in the book,

but even if one concept clicked with you and you recommend
it,

you might just change someone's life around.

We really do not know what people are going through – it's ok
to take a little jump of faith and recommend this book.

Think of this book as a:

- *Small present for birthdays, wedding anniversaries or
  "I love you"!*

- *Tool to have some intellectually stimulating
  conversations at a Party or at work*

- *Something to gift to a book lover*

- *Something to gift to a book non-lover!*

- *Cheer up tool for someone who's ill*

- *Coffee table keep – it sure does have a catchy
  headline!*

Treat the book with the love that it deserves.

I can promise you; the book will love you back like you can never ever imagine!

My Intention For This Book

As you will agree, this book is written straight from the heart. Unfiltered.

Whatever came through, so it is here.

Is has been an absolute honor for me to be used for His work; to be able to receive the messages and pen them down. I do not take this lightly.

My intention for this book is…

Thank you God for making…

- *this book become a best seller and reach each and every bookstore in the whole wide world;*

- *Every Kindle on the planet be graced by this book;*

- *It comes up in discussions at tea conversations in all the roadside cafes;*

- *Talk shows invite me and Manpreet to illustrate the concepts and share our story, starting with TedX;*

- *We do seminars across the world to spread this message;*

- *People get attracted to these principles and apply them in their lives, our social media handles are filled with amazing success stories from all continents;*

- *A little revolution has been unleashed;*

- *A movie is being made on this, with some of the biggest names in entertainment industry working for free, since they believe in the cause…*

Thank you God for making all this and more happen each and every day, in Your time, spirit and energy.

Thank you, thank you, thank you!!!

About the author

Savinder Puri is a software professional, with rich global experience of over two decades, having worked in UK, Europe, South Africa and USA.

He is a recognised figure in the DevOps space and has been speaking at leading industry events worldwide. He has been recognised  as *"10 most dynamic leaders to watch in 2021"* by Business Sight.

Savinder authored the widely popular book *"How do I build a career in DevOps?"*, available on Amazon worldwide. He often talks about technology and Spirituality on his **YouTube channel** – *"DevOps, with a dash of Spirituality"*.

In this lifetime, Savinder's soul mate and spouse Manpreet had a series of health challenges and they both gravitated towards Spirituality to find a deeper meaning to this conundrum called *"life"* and its higher purpose.

Along the way, Savinder became a *Reiki Grandmaster*, *Angelic Healer* and completed an advanced course in *"Expansion of Psychic Abilities"*, *certified by the British Association of the study of Spirituality and Metaphysics (BASSM).*